A RAFT
OF
RIDDLES

A RAFT OF RIDDLES

by Giulio Maestro

E. P. DUTTON • NEW YORK

Library of Congress Cataloging in Publication Data
Maestro, Giulio.   A raft of riddles.

Summary: Answers such questions as "What do trees
drink at parties?" and "What games do eggs play?"
1. Riddles, Juvenile.   [1. Riddles]   I. Title.
PN6371.5.M28   1982   818'.5402   82-2402
ISBN: 0-525-44017-8   AACR2

Published in the United States by E. P. Dutton, Inc.,
2 Park Avenue, New York, N.Y. 10016

Published simultaneously in Canada by Clarke,
Irwin & Company Limited, Toronto and Vancouver

Editor: Ann Durell   Designer: Giulio Maestro

Printed and bound in Hong Kong
by South China Printing Co.
First Edition   10 9 8 7 6 5 4 3 2 1

for Riki

What do trees drink at parties?
Root beer.

Why did the whisk get arrested?
For beating up eggs.

When does an inventor need
an umbrella?

When he gets caught in a brainstorm.

Why did the lock say thank you?
The key had done him a good turn.

Why did the mail carrier win a prize?
She was letter-perfect.

What vegetable can tie your stomach in knots?

String beans.

How does Santa keep the fire hot?
He burns peppermint sticks.

What is small, red, and whispers?
A hoarse radish.

How do bees go to school?
They take the buzz.

What do young lemons recite?
Nursery rinds.

How do bees cut wood?
With a buzz saw.

When is a strawberry like a cucumber?
When one is in a jam and the other is in a pickle.

What games do eggs play?
Softboil and hardboil.

What vegetables have
a college education?
Harvard beets.

What do you call angry rabbits
in summer?

Hot cross bunnies.

Where do twin fruits grow?
On a pair tree.

What did the ladybug say when the fly asked her for a date?

"Gnats to you!"

What is a pickle when he takes his armor off?

A gherkin in a jerkin.

What does a fly wear on a date?
A gnatty outfit.

Why do millionaires find it hard
work to hold on to their money?

It's very taxing.

What does a baby pig like to hug?
A teddy boar.

What do you call a lion who eats ice cubes?

A cool cat.

What happens when a shellfish
is questioned?

He's likely to clam up.

What has feathers, a big mouth, and sits a lot?

A stool pigeon.

What does an oyster bring home from school?

Little pearls of wisdom.

Why was the queen all wet?
Her reign had lasted many years.

What is a lobster's role
in a baseball game?
Relief pincher.

Where does an army of fish sleep?
Under General Anesthesia.

Why did the crab walk to first base?
It was hit by a wild pinch.

What do you call an army officer
who tells bad jokes?

A colonel of corn.

What makes a loaf of bread happy?
Being kneaded.

Who is best at passing meatballs?
A foodball player.

What did the horse say when the farmer painted its stable?

"Now that's a house of a different color!"

How do grapes usually feel?
Vine and dandy.

What do you call a wolf
in sheep's clothing?

A big baa wolf.

How did the apple's new red coat fit?
Just ripe.

What happens when chickens play baseball?

They keep hitting fowl balls.

When is an apple nasty?
When he's rotten to the core.

How can you tell if a hurricane
is happy?
You hear gales of laughter.

Why can't you trust a tree?
It's a shady character.

How does the sun feel about shining?
It's all in a ray's work.

Why did the tow truck speed to the accident?

It was wreckless.

Why was the fruit tree sad?
He was always getting picked on.

When is a pot boiling mad?
When it won't simmer down.

How do beetles travel?
By buggy.

How can you run and stay still
at the same time?

Just stand fast.

What is small, white, fluffy,
and barks?

Pupcorn.

What do you do when your airplane
runs out of gas?

Try not to let it get you down.

How can you find a dogwood tree
in the dark?

Just listen for its bark.

Why did the fish stop eating worms?

She was afraid of getting hooked on them.

How can you spot a shaggy-dog
story?

By the length of its tale.

What happens when two electric
eels meet?

A shocking experience.

How can you split a dog biscuit?
Arf and arf.

How do you clean diamonds and pearls?

Give them a bauble bath.

What vegetable is white and barks?
Collie-flower.

When is money tired?
When it's spent.

What does a house painter do
when it's cold?

She puts on a second coat.

What kind of jokes do fish tell?
Very finny ones!